Step 1
Go to **www.openlightbox.com**

Step 2
Enter this unique code
UIXQG3KVH

Step 3
Explore your interactive eBook!

Your interactive eBook comes with...

Audio
Listen to the entire book read aloud

Videos
Watch informative video clips

Weblinks
Gain additional information for research

Try This!
Complete activities and hands-on experiments

Key Words
Study vocabulary, and complete a matching word activity

Quizzes
Test your knowledge

Slideshows
View images and captions

Share
Share titles within your Learning Management System (LMS) or Library Circulation System

Citation
Create bibliographical references following APA, CMOS, and MLA styles

This title is part of our AV2 digital subscription

1-Year K–2 Subscription
ISBN 978-1-7911-3310-8

Access hundreds of AV2 titles with our digital subscription.
Sign up for a FREE trial at **www.openlightbox.com/trial**

The digital components of this book are guaranteed to stay active for at least five years from the date of publication.

Rottweiler

CONTENTS

- 2 Interactive eBook Code
- 4 Loyal and Confident
- 6 Large Dogs
- 8 Coat Colors
- 10 Growing Up
- 12 Working Dogs
- 14 Exercise
- 16 Grooming
- 18 Food and Attention
- 20 Staying Healthy
- 22 Incredible Rottweilers
- 24 Sight Words

My rottweiler is loyal and wants to protect our family.

He is confident in his strength.

Rottweilers are large dogs. They are strong and very powerful.

Dog Shoulder Heights

German Shepherd
Up to 26 inches
(66 centimeters)

Rottweiler
Up to 27 inches
(69 cm)

Doberman Pinscher
Up to 28 inches
(71 cm)

All rottweilers have black coats with markings. My dog's markings are tan.

Other rottweilers may have rust or mahogany markings.

Rottweiler puppies are smart. They can be trained early.

They should meet new people and dogs as they grow up.

Where in the World

Rottweilers come from German dogs that used to herd cattle and pull carts.

Rottweilers are hard workers.

Some may guard homes, work on farms, or even help the police.

My rottweiler needs plenty of exercise.

We go on long walks.

I let him run around to burn energy.

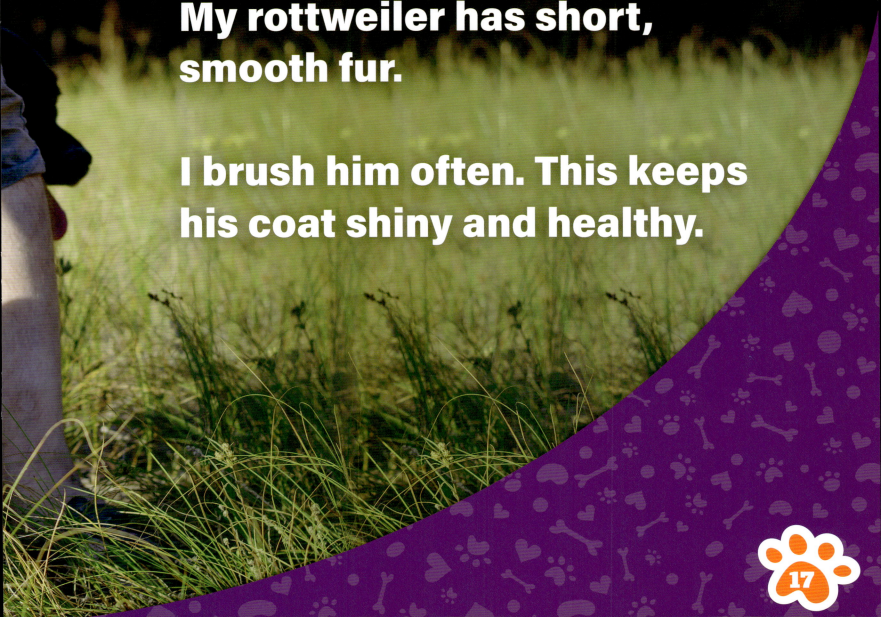

My rottweiler has short, smooth fur.

I brush him often. This keeps his coat shiny and healthy.

I feed my rottweiler twice a day.

I also play with him often.
His favorite game is tug of war.

I take my rottweiler to the veterinarian at least once a year.

The veterinarian helps keep my dog healthy.

Dog Breed Popularity in the United States

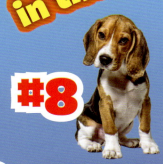
#8
Beagle

#9
Rottweiler

#10
German Shorthaired Pointer

Incredible Rottweilers

Most rottweilers weigh about **80** to **135 pounds** (36 to 61 kilograms).

Rottweilers are one of the best **guard dog** breeds.

About **6** to **12 puppies** are born in most rottweiler litters.

Rottweilers are among the **oldest** herding breeds.

SIGHT WORDS

Research has shown that as much as 65 percent of all written material published in English is made up of 300 words. These 300 words cannot be taught using pictures or learned by sounding them out. They must be recognized by sight. This book contains 65 common sight words to help young readers improve their reading fluency and comprehension. This book also teaches young readers several important content words, such as proper nouns. These words are paired with pictures to aid in learning and improve understanding.

Page	Sight Words First Appearance
4	and, family, he, his, in, is, my, our, to, wants
6	are, large, they, up, very
9	all, have, may, or, other, with
10	be, can
11	as, come, from, grow, new, people, should, that, the, where, world
12	even, farms, hard, help, homes, on, some, work
14	go, long, needs, of, walks, we
15	around, him, I, let, run
17	keeps, often, this
18	a, day
19	also, play
20	at, once, states, take, year

Page	Content Words First Appearance
4	rottweiler, strength
6	Doberman pinscher, dogs, German shepherd, heights, shoulder
9	coats, markings
10	puppies
11	carts, cattle
12	police, workers
14	exercise
15	energy
17	fur
19	game, tug of war
20	beagle, breed, German shorthaired pointer, popularity, United States, veterinarian

Published by Lightbox Learning Inc.
276 5th Avenue, Suite 704 #917
New York, NY 10001
Website: www.openlightbox.com

Copyright ©2026 Lightbox Learning Inc.
All rights reserved. No part of this publication may be reproduced, stored in a retrieval system, or transmitted in any form or by any means, electronic, mechanical, photocopying, recording, or otherwise, without the prior written permission of the publisher.

Library of Congress Control Number: 2024057380

ISBN 979-8-8745-2150-9 (hardcover)
ISBN 979-8-8745-2148-6 (softcover)
ISBN 979-8-8745-2149-3 (static multi-user eBook)
ISBN 979-8-8745-2152-3 (interactive multi-user eBook)

012025
100924

Printed in Guangzhou, China
1 2 3 4 5 6 7 8 9 0   29 28 27 26 25

Project Coordinator: Priyanka Das
Designer: Jean Faye Rodriguez

Every reasonable effort has been made to trace ownership and to obtain permission to reprint copyright material. The publisher would be pleased to have any errors or omissions brought to its attention so that they may be corrected in subsequent printings.

The publisher acknowledges Getty Images and Shutterstock as its primary image suppliers for this title.